THREE

Ceremonial Pieces

for Organ

edited by Carson Cooman

Table of Contents

Editedby Carson Cooman

H. T. FitzSimons Company

Exclusively Distributed by

Hal • Leonard

to my teacher, Donald McDonald, with great admiration

Trumpet Pastorale

Sw. Flute 8, Celeste
Gt. Trumpet or Oboe
Ped. Soft 16, 8, Sw. to Ped.

Richard E. Frey
(1970)

Gt. (or Ch.): Flutes 8, 2
15
Gt. (Ch.)
20
Gt. (Tpt. or Oboe)
(Sw.)
24
3
28
3
rit.

Processional for Organ

Warren Martin
(1955)

Rather slowly (♩ = ca. 63)

19
3rd time to Coda
(2nd time, rit.)
Solo
sim.
24
28
32
take repeat twice
Coda

Processional Music

for a Solemn and Joyous Occasion

Kenneth Mahy
(1964)

Andante maestoso (♩ = ca. 80)

* For a shortened version of this piece, play the manual parts only in this measure (22), then cut to measure 55.

23
Gt. mf
Sw. mf
mf
28
3
3
32
36

* For an extended version of this piece, a return to the beginning may be made upon completion of this measure (47).

55
Gt. ff
Sw. ff
ff
59
3
5
3
63
67
rit.

Notes on the Composers and Works

Richard E. Frey (b. 1945) was educated at Westminster Choir College, Boston University, and Palmer Theological Seminary. His first composition teacher was Warren Martin. He has served as organist and director of music at a number of churches. As a composer, Frey has published compositions with various firms, including the H. T. Fitzsimmons Co., Hope Publishing, and Lorenz Publishing Co.

Trumpet Pastorale was composed in 1970 and is dedicated to Frey's teacher Donald McDonald, who was organ professor at Westminster Choir College for 42 years.

Warren Martin (1916–1982) is best known for his long association with Westminster Choir College. He entered the college in 1932 at the age of 15 and graduated in 1936, earning bachelor's and master's degrees. After major posts in Los Angeles (First Congregational Church) and Chicago (Rockefeller Chapel at the University of Chicago), Martin returned to Westminster in 1950, where he was a member of the faculty for more than 30 years, until his death. During his tenure he served as head of graduate studies, conductor of the Symphonic and Westminster Choirs, and professor of composition and theory. Among Martin's best known works is the comic oratorio ***The True Story of Cinderella*** (1955).

Processional for Organ was composed in 1955 at the request of John Finley Williamson and, along with Martin's choral work ***Anthem of Dedication***, remains a traditional part of Westminster's commencement exercises.

Kenneth Mahy (b. 1937) was born in China to missionary parents and spent most of his childhood in China and the Philippines. Upon his family's return to the United States, Mahy attended Westminster Choir College as a voice major. After earning his bachelor's degree, he joined the United States Navy and spent four years as a chorus member and baritone soloist with the Navy Band Sea Chanters in Washington, D.C. Mahy pursued graduate studies in composition with George Thaddeus Jones at Catholic University of America, earning a master's degree in composition in 1963. After holding several teaching positions and earning a doctorate in vocal performance and literature from Indiana University (1974), Mahy joined the faculty of West Liberty State College (West Virginia) where he remained active as teacher, composer, and performer until his retirement in 2002. The bulk of Mahy's output consists of vocal and choral music, most of it stemming from his own extensive experience as a performer and voice teacher.

Processional Music (for a Solemn and Joyous Occasion) is Mahy's only work for solo organ. It was composed in 1964 for the composer's own wedding to his wife, Jill.

H. T. FitzSimons Company
Exclusively Distributed by
Hal•Leonard

THREE Ceremonial Pieces for Organ

edited by Carson Cooman

Carson Cooman (b. 1982) is an American composer with a catalog of hundreds of works in many forms—from solo instrumental pieces to operas, and from orchestral works to hymn tunes. His music has been performed on all six inhabited continents in venues that range from the stage of Carnegie Hall to the basket of a hot air balloon. Cooman's music appears on over forty recordings, including more than twenty complete CDs on the Naxos, Albany, Artek, Gothic, Divine Art, Métier, Diversions, Convivium, Altarus, MSR Classics, Raven, and Zimbel labels. Cooman's primary composition studies were with Bernard Rands, Judith Weir, Alan Fletcher, and James Willey. As an active concert organist, Cooman specializes in the performance of contemporary music. Over 150 new compositions by more than 100 international composers have been written for him, and his organ performances can be heard on a number of CD recordings. Cooman is also a writer on musical subjects, producing articles and reviews frequently for a number of international publications. He serves as an active consultant on music business matters to composers and performing organizations, specializing particularly in the area of composer estates and archives. Since 2015, he has been organ editor for Lorenz Publishing Co./Sacred Music Press. For more information, visit www.carsoncooman.com.

H. T. FITZSIMONS COMPANY
EXCLUSIVELY DISTRIBUTED BY
HAL•LEONARD